War in the Gulf

OPERATION DESERT STORM

Written By: Paul J. Deegan

Published by Abdo & Daughters, 6535 Cecilia Circle, Edina, Minnesota 55439.

Library bound edition distributed by Rockbottom Books, Pentagon Tower, P.O. Box 36036, Minneapolis, Minnesota 55435.

Library of Congress Number: 91-073078   ISBN: 1-56239-023-6

Cover Photo by: Bettmann
Inside Photos by: Reuters/Bettmann: 4, 7, 8, 13, 17, 27, 28, 31, 35, 37, 38,
                    41, 44
                    UPI/Bettmann: 19, 24, 48
                    Globe Photos: 15
                    Official U.S. Air Force: 20

Edited by: Rosemary Wallner

TABLE OF CONTENTS

U.S. servicemen and a Saudi Arabian citizen share a cup of tea during the gulf war build-up.

UNWAVERING FRIENDSHIP

"The United States of America has shown unwavering friendship through its resolve to uphold the principles of the United Nations and secure justice over the fate of Kuwait.

"The men and women of the U.S. Forces in the Gulf have played a vital role in coming to the aid of a small nation at the mercy of a ruthless and vicious neighbor.

"For this generous response, in the true spirit of freedom, the people of Kuwait are profoundly grateful to every single one of you.

"When the time came the people of America have proved to be true friends of a nation in desperate need.

"We thank you.

　　　　"From the People of Kuwait"

This advertisement appeared in the March 11, 1991, issue of a major United States news magazine. The headline on the ad said: "True Colors of Friendship."

The United States befriended Kuwait, a country in the Persian Gulf, by sending over half-a-million troops to fight in the desert halfway around the world. The U.S. organized and orchestrated Operation Desert Storm, the largest invasion force assembled in half a century. The primarily American force also included troops from 28 other nations participating in the coalition lined up against Iraq, Kuwait's much larger neighbor.

The American troops had been sent to Saudi Arabia after Iraq invaded Kuwait on August 2, 1990. The same day, the United Nations Security Council condemned the invasion. Four days later President George Bush sent the first troops and airplanes to the Persian Gulf under Operation Desert Shield. On November 29, 1990, the Security Council passed a resolution saying "all necessary means" could be used to remove Iraqi forces from Kuwait if they hadn't voluntarily left by January 15, 1991.

Iraq's President Saddam Hussein did not withdraw his troops from Kuwait by the deadline. Saddam had refused to voluntarily give up Kuwait despite the pleas of diplomats worldwide. So on

January 16, 1991, President Bush ordered the start of an air attack aimed at forcing Iraq to withdraw.

That night, White House Press Secretary Marlin Fitzwater announced that, "The liberation of Kuwait has begun." Operation Desert Shield had become Operation Desert Storm.

The long-discussed land war followed 39 days later. After only 100 hours, coalition forces routed the much-feared Iraqi military. Only 124 of the United States troops in the campaign died.

U.S. President George Bush

Iraq's President Saddam Hussein

F-117 "Stealth" fighter sits at an airbase in Saudi Arabia. The Stealth played a key role in the air war against Iraq.

ASSAULT FROM THE SKY

Operation Desert Storm began with the most powerful air assault in history. It was also a startling display of modern military technology. New "high-tech" war machinery got its first use in this conflict. Among the modern weapons were:

- Tomahawk cruise missiles that were preprogrammed to their targets.

- F-117A "Stealth" fighters dropping "smart bombs."

- Patriot antimissile systems.

- F-46 Wild Weasel aircraft with radar-sensing and radar-jamming equipment.

- Laser-guided artillery shells directed at enemy artillery and tanks.

The first weapons launched in the air war were the Tomahawk missiles. Twenty feet long, the missiles compare radar images of the ground over which they fly to maps preprogrammed into their computer memories. They fly as low as 100 feet from the ground. It is almost impossible to defend against them.

The first wave of planes to attack under Operation Desert Storm was made up of 30 Lockheed F-117A fighters. The Stealth was a weapon most people knew nothing about because it was designed and developed in secrecy. The plane, shaped like an arrowhead, has a super-modern look. Each Stealth cost over $46 million.

Each Stealth dropped two, 2,000-pound bombs. These laser-directed glide bombs were called "smart bombs" because they can fix upon and destroy a very specific target. With these "smart bombs," anything that can be seen from the air can be blown up.

One target for the Stealths was the Iraqi Air Force headquarters. Reportedly, one of the bombs was so accurate that it entered the building's cooling system and blew up the building.

The U.S. and allied pilots flew over 1,000 sorties — air missions — in the first 24 hours of Operation Desert Storm. They flew over 4,700 in the first week, losing only 10 planes.

I MISS YOU

The beginning of the Persian Gulf War increased the concern of the families of the men and women doing the fighting. The mothers and fathers, wives and husbands, sisters and brothers, daughters and sons on both sides of the conflict worried about the safe return of their loved ones.

A Minnesota woman wrote her Marine corporal husband:

"Good night Steve. I miss you. I love you. You're a hero."

He was killed in the war shortly after she wrote the letter.

In a little Tennessee town, a 53-year-old woman saw four sons, ages 20 to 32, go to Saudi Arabia. A fifth son awaited the call-up of his reserve unit.

On a winter Sunday in Iowa, a Lutheran pastor in a Des Moines suburb told his congregation that "every one of these Iraqi guys we see (on television) has a family too."

Despite the worry and concern, polls taken during Operation Desert Storm showed that the American people were firmly behind the president's use of force in the Gulf. But not everyone agreed on the wisdom of his policy. Some wondered aloud if the Bush administration knew what it wanted to do in the area after the war ended. One columnist said the administration had failed "to look beyond the war to consider what kind of peace there can be . . ." Thomas Friedman, the *New York Times* veteran Middle East reporter, likened the war in the Gulf to a square dance. "Who's hand are you going to be holding when the light's come on?" he asked.

IRAQ FIRES AT ISRAEL

On the second day of Desert Storm, Saddam made good on an earlier promise. He fired eight Scud missiles across the country of Jordan into the cities of Tel Aviv and Haifa in Israel. The Israelis, who were not participating in the war, were angry. They informed the United States that they were going to respond militarily.

Prime Minister Shamir of Israel tells the U.S. that he is going to respond militarily for the attack against his country.

Saddam probably hoped that Israel would enter the war. For a long time, Israel and the Arab nations, including Saudi Arabia, an ally of the United States, had been enemies. If Israel entered the war, the Arab soldiers might withdraw from the coalition formed against Saddam Hussein. The Israeli-Arab conflict would then have broken up the coalition.

To keep Israel from striking back against Iraq, the Bush administration rushed a new weapon, Patriot air defense missiles, to Israel. The radio-commanded Patriots explode with a proximity fuse when they near an incoming missile. The U.S. also sent along American crews to operate the Patriots.

President Bush also promised Israel that the United States would increase its efforts to find and destroy the Scud launchers within Iraq.

Altogether, Iraq launched 81 Scud attacks before the war ended. About half of them were aimed at sites in Saudi Arabia. Many times, however, the Patriots intercepted and destroyed the Scuds.

Patriot Missle, the weapon that gave the U.S. the edge.

MOST BOMBS EVER

By January 30, the aerial assault had become the most massive two-week bombing campaign the world had ever known. By February 4, day 20 of Operation Desert Storm, U.S. officials said over 40,000 sorties had been directed against Iraq. In comparison, during the last *14 months* of World War II, only 30,000 missions were flown against Japan. The total number of sorties flown by allied planes during Operation Desert Storm was 110,000.

Iraq's capital and largest city, Baghdad, already had been repeatedly attacked. U.S. military leaders emphasized that they were "scrupulously avoiding civilian targets." President Bush said repeatedly that the U.S. had no quarrel with the Iraqi people, only Saddam Hussein.

The focus of the air war was to destroy equipment and supplies. A national security expert said the United States was "not trying to kill people." He added that the aerial attacks were intended to soften the 500,000-plus Iraqi forces in southern Iraq and Kuwait. Fewer Iraqi troops would reduce allied casualties in the anticipated land invasion to retake Kuwait.

Service crew gives "thumbs up" to pilots in their jets as they prepare to take off.

Iraqi communications centers, military command posts, and important military installations such as airfields, aircraft bunkers, ammunition depots, and oil-pumping stations were the targets of allied planes. So too were supply lines linking Baghdad with the Iraqi troops to the south. Roads and bridges throughout Iraq were destroyed. The Iraqis were thought to have built a network of roads in Kuwait and these, too, were heavily bombed by the allies.

Power and water plants were among the non-military sites targeted for destruction. So was the civilian telephone system. American public health specialists who went to Iraq in April 1991 said the destroyed public utility systems had created severe problems incuding the possibility of starvation and the spread of contagious diseases.

The heavy bombing of such major Iraqi cities as Baghdad and Basra in the south produced civilian casualties although postwar visitors said housing damage was minimal. During the war, the U.S. military referred to civilian casualties as "modest collateral damage." No details ever were available on the number of Iraqi civilians killed or wounded.

A spokesman at the Pentagon in Washington, D.C., said, "There simply isn't any way of knowing." Estimates by those outside the government ranged from a few thousand Iraqi dead to more than 10,000.

American casualties in the air war were light. After four weeks, only 14 were dead and 12 wounded. U.S. Defense Secretary Dick Cheney praised the pilots as the "heart and soul" of the most successful air attack in history.

B-52 bomber

U.S. TARGETS
REPUBLICAN GUARD UNITS

A particular target of the allied air war was Iraq's Republican Guard units. These troops were supposed to be Iraq's best-trained and best-equipped forces. They were organized as heavily armored, very mobile units. They were stationed near Iraq's border with northwestern Kuwait. Huge U.S. B-52 bombers hammered the Guards to lessen their effectiveness in case of a possible allied land invasion.

Iraqi air forces were seldom a factor in the war. They stayed on the ground in the first allied air attacks. Later a few ventured into the air and several were shot down. In the last week of January, Iraqi pilots began landing planes in Iran, Iraq's western neighbor and opponent in a 1980-1988 war. Iran had declared itself neutral in the Gulf War. No one was sure why the planes went to Iran, but within a few days some 90 planes had landed there.

A U.S. general in Saudi Arabia said one-third of Iraq's air force may have been eliminated in the bombing. This figure came from adding destroyed planes to those that were flown to shelter in Iran.

$500 MILLION A DAY

Once the war was underway, it was estimated that the cost of the war to the United States was perhaps $500 million *a day*. Almost three weeks into Operation Desert Storm, the White House budget director, Richard Darman, said the administration was forecasting that the war would cost $66 billion. There were no plans to raise taxes to pay for the war according to the administration.

Darman said the U.S. government believed the allies would pay $51 billion of the total cost. The major share of this, $41.5 billion, was expected to be paid by four countries: Kuwait and Saudi Arabia each would pay $13.5 billion, Japan would pay $9 billion, and Germany would pay $5.5 billion. These sums would pay what was then estimated to be the costs of three months of fighting, twice as long as the war actually lasted.

The U.S. Congress pressured the administration to seek larger contributions from Japan and Germany. These countries are dependent on Persian Gulf oil, but did not commit ground forces to Operation Desert Storm.

OIL SPILLS INTO GULF

The conflict in the Persian Gulf produced problems in the sea itself. Large oil spills into the gulf created the specter of terrible damage to the environment and threatened the drinking supplies of Gulf nations.

The largest spill was first estimated at seven million barrels of oil. It came from Kuwait's offshore Sea Island Terminal when the occupying Iraqis opened the taps on this supertanker loading dock. They also drained the oil from five nearby Kuwaiti tanker ships. Later experts determined that the spill was actually much less — perhaps one million barrels. Another 500,000 barrels leaked from storage tanks along the coast after allied planes had bombed Iraqi targets.

The Saudis set up huge flotation booms to protect facilities in Jubail, a city on Saudi Arabia's Persian Gulf coast. The facilities included water purification plants and electricity-generating stations. The main water purification plant at Jubail provides nearly half of Saudi Arabia's drinking water. If the oil spills reached shore, Jubail's plants might become contaminated. The Saudis would lack clean water to drink.

Although the oil spills were slowed, it will take time before the full extent of the damage to the gulf's ecosystem can be determined.

U.S. Secretary of Defense Richard Cheney examines a map during a briefing by Brig. Gen. Ed Scholes (right), commander of the Army 18th Airborne Corps.

WOULD THERE BE A GROUND WAR?

In the first part of February 1991, Secretary Cheney traveled to Saudi Arabia with General Colin Powell, chairman of the Joint Chiefs of Staff. The two U.S. military leaders went to the Gulf for a brief inspection tour.

A major focus of their tour concerned a possible ground invasion of Kuwait. President Bush had said repeatedly that no decision had been made about launching a land war in the Gulf. But Cheney's comments on the trip indicated that he believed that some sort of ground attack would be necessary.

The defense secretary talked to the U.S. airmen and women about the need to make Iraqi troops abandon their dug-in positions so they would be easier targets for the pilots. Cheney said that attacks by soldiers and Marines moving on the ground and from the sea could flush out the Iraqi forces.

Powell told the U.S.troops that he, too, favored using ground troops "to make air power even that much more effective." The combination, he said, would shorten the war.

In the United States, many pople worried about the possibility of massive American casualties if the troops became involved in a direct, full-out ground attack in the Gulf. Addressing that issue, Powell told the troops that casualties could be held to acceptable levels. He said a ground campaign did not assure "huge casualties."

Meanwhile, the first Iraqi forces had moved into Saudi Arabia from their dug-in positions in Kuwait. Four days later, the first U.S. ground troops were killed in the war. Seven Marines were killed by "friendly fire." A missile, probably fired by a U.S. Air Force aircraft, struck the Marine's light armored vehicle. The Marines had been battling a column of Iraqi tanks and armored personnel carriers.

While Cheney and Powell were in Saudi Arabia, a U.S. Marine scout team went into Kuwait. The *Wisconsin*, a U.S. battleship from World War II, pounded the Kuwaiti coast with 1,900-pound shells to create a diversion for the Marines. The *Wisconsin* was about a half-mile off shore in the Persian Gulf. It was the first time since the 1950s Korean War that the ship's guns were fired in battle.

Three of the USS Wisconsin's *16-inch guns were pointed in the direction of the Kuwaiti Coast.*

General Norman Schwarzkopf, commander in chief of the U.S. forces, replies to questions during a news conference.

BUSH SAYS GO

In February 1991, the Soviet Union tried to negotiate Iraq's withdrawal from Kuwait. The effort failed and a ground war now seemed inevitable. President Bush had to make the decision. On February 22, a public television commentator said of Operation Desert Storm, "It's been a show run and called by Bush." At midday the following day, President Bush gave General H. Norman Schwarzkopf, the commander of allied forces in the Gulf, the go-ahead to begin the ground war.

The allied ground assault began under cover of darkness at 4 a.m. local time on Sunday, February 24, 1991. (It was still Saturday night in the United States.) American forces were joined by the troops of nine other nations. The allied armies incuded the tank corps of the U.S. 7th Corps, the British "Desert Rats," and the French Foreign Legion.

Iraq's ground forces were hunkered down in bunkers that they had spent months digging.

Iraq's long-range artillery was said to be highly effective. The Iraqi army's firepower also included Soviet-built tanks and other armor, anti-tank weapons, and machine guns. A fierce battle was anticipated.

Instead, U.S. and coalition forces watched in amazement as Iraqi soldiers, pounded by six weeks of allied air assault, happily surrendered by the thousands. There was no resistance to the U.S. attack on Iraq's first line of defense in Kuwait. Many of the Iraqi soldiers in the front lines were conscripts. The punishing air bombardment had been enough for these Iraqi recruits. They were also starving; the bombing had cut off their food supplies. They abandoned their tanks and surrendered. "Some of them were barefoot," said one American soldier. "They were all scared."

Iraqi field officers told U.S. military people after the war that they were stunned when the allied invasion began. The Iraqi officers never thought there would be a ground war. One U.S. official said the Iraqis "thought Saddam was playing a game of chicken and would turn off the road at the last minute."

When he didn't, the Iraqi field commanders were left unprepared. They also were severely handicapped because the air war had cut their lines of communication with Baghdad.

Many surrendering soldiers told the allied troops that their officers had abandoned them when the fighting began. General Schwarzkopf said he put much of the blame on the Iraqi army's failure to fight "on their own leadership. They committed them to a cause they did not believe in."

The Iraqi army was stunned when the allied invasion began.

A RELUCTANT FOE

"It was an army without a battle plan. Its soldiers did not want to fight." This was *Newsday's* comments about the Iraqi army. The feared Iraqi forces mounted almost no opposition during the first two days of the 100-hour ground war. The U.S. forces advanced into Kuwait without, for the most part, ever firing a shot. Most allied units had no casualties.

"A football game would be over very quickly if the other team decided not to play," General Schwarzkopf, the allied commander, said on public television in late March. "And," he added, "that's what happened" when the American-led forces started the ground war. "The United States," the general said, "came to play."

Iraq had entered the war with 4,200 tanks. By February 27, the last day of the war, at least 3,000 had been destroyed, according to Gen. Schwarzkopf. He said this did not include several hundred more tanks manned by Iraq's Republican Guards. These tanks were involved in the war's final battle, a fierce clash of men and machinery in the biggest tank battle since World War II. This battle took place near Basra, 30 miles north of

Kuwait. Eight Republican Guard divisions, the pride of Saddam's Army, were routed in the fighting.

As the brief ground campaign neared its end, the Iraqi troops who hadn't surrendered were disorganized and tried to flee to safety. They used cars, buses, and military and civilian trucks in their attempt to reach and cross the Euphrates River, which runs north to south in central Iraq. Iraqi vehicles were backed up for miles on roads heading north out of Kuwait City and in southern Iraq.

Several weeks after the war, there were reports that the retreating troops, some flying white flags on their vehicles, were bombed and attacked by United States planes and ground troops. Some Americans on the scene called it a "turkey shoot." Ruined civilian vehicles littered the highway from Kuwait to Baghdad.

Some in the U.S. military described the killing of Iraqi soldiers who were not fighting as an excessive use of force. "An outrage," said one. But others said "very brutal things" take place in a war. General Schwarzkopf said in a late television interview that he had recommended continuing the allied march into Iraq. "We had them in a rout," he said, and "we could have continued to . . . wreak great destruction upon them." The general said the allied forces could have "made it in fact a battle of annihilation."

After his remarks caused anger in the White House, General Schwarzkopf later said he was talking about an initial plan and not what he had recommended to the president.

In Washington on February 27, 1991, President Bush was told by his military advisers that the battle was won. American, British, and French forces had advanced to within 150 miles of Baghdad. The president announced that he was calling an end to the fighting as of midnight, Eastern Standard Time, on the 27th. "Kuwait is liberated," the president said. "Iraq's army is defeated."

Operation Desert Storm was over 42 days after it began. British Lieutenant. General Peter de la Billiere called it "one of the greatest victories . . . experienced in our lives and possibly in history."

The allied forces advance to within 150 miles of Baghdad.

A LOVE AFFAIR

During Operation Desert Storm, a love affair developed between the American people and the U.S. forces fighting in the Gulf. The troops' "simple dedication" to the task at hand "was as impressive as their technical skill," a newspaper columnist noted. The troops' determination to succeed was applauded. Feelings of patriotism reached heights not seen in this country since World War II in the 1940s.

Military professionals, too, felt good about the successful war. Addressing a Veterans of Foreign Wars convention right after fighting ceased in the Gulf War, General Powell said, "It's great to have a clean win, isn't it?"

Powell praised President Bush for having given "clear, unmistakable policy directions" to the military. He said the president understood that "there is no substitute for victory."

The general also praised General Schwarzkopf, who directed the war from U.S. Central Command in Riyadh, Saudi Arabia. Powell said the president was "very fortunate to have "Stormin' Norman" in charge."

General Norman Schwarzkopf - "Stormin' Norman."

Gen. Schwarzkopf and his theater commanders were lauded after the war for their strategy in planning the overwhelmingly successful land war. Their plan included moving some 200,000 troops to western Saudi Arabia from where they flanked the Iraqi army when the ground fighting began.

Speaking on public television after the war ended, Gen. Schwarzkopf said that as "an idealist" he believed "there are some things worth fighting for — family, liberty, and freedom."

U.S. AND IRAQI CASUALTIES

There are no reliable figures on the number of Iraqi troops killed during Operation Desert Storm. Rough estimates place the number to about 100,000. There had been, according to estimates, over 400,000 Iraqi troops in or near Kuwait at one time.

U.S. military leaders estimated that some 60,000 to 75,000 Iraqi soldiers were taken prisoner. The majority of them had surrendered. After the war, they were returned to Iraq unless they refused to go.

Amazingly, the total combat death of U.S. soldiers was only 124. When the war action halted, eight American men and one American woman were prisoners of war. All were released a few days later. There were also 45 Americans listed as missing in action.

Gen. Schwarzkopf congratulates his troops on their victory in the Persian Gulf War.

UNREST IN KUWAIT

Before retreating from Kuwait, Iraqi forces set fire to more than half of Kuwait's 1,000 oil wells. The burning wells, an observer said, "turned the noon sun into twilight." The dollar value of the burning oil was said to be $80 million a day. No one knew how long it would take to put out the fires. Firefighters from the United States were brought to Kuwait to do the job.

Reporters moving into Kuwait after Kuwait City was liberated reported that most of the country was trashed, looted, and burned by Iraqi troops.

There also were reports that thousands of Kuwaitis had been executed by Iraqis during their occupation of Kuwait. However, these charges could not be proved after the war.

But the brutality of Iraqi torture of Kuwaitis was documented. The great anger aroused by this mistreatment was a factor in the Kuwaitis attacking foreign residents, particularly Palestinians, after the war. These non-Kuwaitis were suspected of having collaborated with the Iraqis during the occupation.

The Emir of Kuwait Government Palace, gutted and burned by the Iraqis.

WHEN WOULD THE SOLDIERS COME HOME?

When the war ended on February 27, the soldiers and their relatives had one big question. When would the 540,000 American fighting men and women be coming home? Actually, withdrawal plans hadn't been formed because the fighting had ended much quicker than expected. Secretary of State Cheney did say it could be November 1991 before the last of the troops came home. He said those who had first been sent to Saudi Arabia would be the first returned.

By April 10, 1991, over one-third of the U.S. troops sent to the Persian Gulf had returned home. But as April began, over a month after President Bush ordered an end to the fighting, U.S. troops in southern Iraq still controlled about 15 percent of the country.

Soldiers at the northernmost U.S. observation post, about 150 miles into Iraq, watched in late March 1991 as Iraqi Republican Guard troops attacked Iraqi Shiite Moslems in a nearby town during the civil rebellion in Iraq. The rebellion also involved a Kurdish uprising in the north of Iraq.

The Bush administration wanted to keep American troops out of the postwar conflict. The president said U.S. soldiers would not participate in an Iraqi civil war.

However, on April 16, 1991, President Bush sent U.S. soldiers into northern Iraq. Along with British and French troops, they were to establish secure camps to shelter displaced Kurds who had fled their towns and villages. Some 1.5 million of Iraq's four million Kurds were massed near Iraq's border with Turkey or had crossed over the border to Iran.

Exiled Kurdish refugee's.

CEASE-FIRE IMPLEMENTED

After President Bush ordered an end to the fighting, work began on a permanent cease-fire to formally end Operation Desert Storm. The first step took place on Sunday, March 3, 1991, when General Schwarzkopf met with Iraqi military commanders in U.S.-occupied southern Iraq. The Iraqis agreed to an immediate exchange of all prisoners of war.

Five weeks after the U.S. and its allies drove Iraq's army from Kuwait, Iraq said on April 6 that it accepted the United Nations Security Council's terms for a formal cease-fire. Those terms were spelled out in Resolution 687, passed by the Security Council three days earlier. Iraq's United Nations representative said Iraq accepted the terms "without conditions," but that he considered them "one-sided and unfair."

The cease-fire terms call for Iraq to destroy its chemical and biological weapons and its long-range biological weapons. Nuclear materials that could be used for weapons are also to be removed. Iraq is held liable for war damages, including environmental damage, resulting from its stay in Kuwait.

The United Nations Security Council on April 11 officially declared a cease-fire. The council also approved a 1,440-member peacekeeping force to monitor a 75-mile-long UN buffer zone between Iraq and Kuwait. The zone stretches six miles into Iraq and three miles into Kuwait.

When the first United Nations observers and soldiers moved into the zone April 12, the U.S. began withdrawing its troops from southern Iraq. Most of the American troops in Saudi Arabia also returned to the United States. Among those who stayed were the members of a small Air Force group. The White House said U.S. planes would continue to fly over Iraq to make sure the cease-fire was honored.

******

It was a happy, emotional President Bush who addressed a joint session of Congress on the night of March 6, 1991. Even the opposition party praised him. The speaker of the house, the top majority post in that body, always intoduces the president. Thomas Foley, a Washington Democrat, departed from the usual formal introduction. He congratulated the president "on a brilliant victory in Operation Desert Storm."

That night President Bush told Congress and the nation that U.S. troops fought with "honor and valor." He said:

"We're coming home now — proud, confident, heads high. . . . We are Americans."

President Bush receives applause before addressing a joint session of Congress.